12/08

W9-BSQ-357

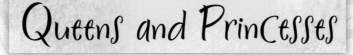

Queens and Princesses

QUEEN
Rania
OF JORDAN

by Mary Englar

Consultant:

Christopher Rose

Assistant Director

Center for Middle Eastern Studies

The University of Texas at Austin

Capstone press®

Mankato, Minnesota

Fossil Ridge Public Library District
Braidwood, IL 60408

Snap Books are published by Capstone Press,
151 Good Counsel Drive, P.O. Box 669, Mankato, Minnesota 56002.
www.capstonepress.com

Library of Congress Cataloging-in-Publication Data
Englar, Mary.
Queen Rania of Jordan / by Mary Englar.
    p. cm. — (Snap books. Queens and princesses)
    Summary: "Describes the life of Queen Rania of Jordan" — Provided by
publisher.
    Includes bibliographical references and index.
    ISBN-13: 978-1-4296-1959-2 (hardcover)
    ISBN-10: 1-4296-1959-7 (hardcover)
    1. Rania, Queen, consort of Abdullah II, King of Jordan, 1970– 2. Queens —
Jordan — Biography. 3. Jordan — Politics and government — 1999– I. Title. II.
Series.
DS154.52.R36E54 2009
956.9504'4092 — dc22   2008000614

Editor: Christine Peterson
Designer: Juliette Peters
Photo Researcher: Wanda Winch

Photo Credits:
AP Images/Eyal Warshavsky, 6; Corbis Sygma/Attar Maher, 5, 16; Getty Images
Inc./AFP, 11; Getty Images Inc./AFP/Christophe Simon, 21 (bottom); Getty Images
Inc./AFP/Jamal Nasrallah, 13; Getty Images Inc./AFP/Khalil Mazraawi, 23; Getty
Images Inc./AFP/Rabih Moghrabi, 12; Getty Images Inc./AFP/Raed Quteina, 9; Getty
Images Inc./Jordanian Royal Palace, 17; Getty Images Inc./Joyce Tenneson, cover;
Getty Images Inc./Tom Stoddart, 15, 29; Landov LLC/dpa/Frank Rumpenhorst, 28;
Landov LLC/Reuters/Ali Jarekji, 21 (top), 26; Landov LLC/Reuters/Brian Snyder, 19;
Landov LLC/Reuters/Laszlo Balogh, 25; Landov LLC/Reuters/Majed Jaber, 7; Landov
LLC/Reuters/Naser Ayoub, 27; Landov LLC/Zuher Omar, 20; Shutterstock/Condor
36, 10

Essential content terms are **bold** and are defined at the bottom of the page where
they appear.

1 2 3 4 5 6 13 12 11 10 09 08

Table of Contents

AN UNEXPECTED
Honor

Rania Al-Yassin never dreamed of becoming a queen. Even after marrying Jordan's Prince Abdullah, Rania didn't expect to hold the royal title of queen. But on the morning of June 9, 1999, Rania was crowned queen of Jordan. At age 28, she was the youngest queen in the world.

Abdullah and Rania felt unprepared. Her husband was now known as King Abdullah II. He was the country's first new king in 47 years. His father, King Hussein, had ruled Jordan until his death earlier that year. Just two weeks before he died, King Hussein decided that Abdullah should succeed him as Jordan's leader.

The royal couple's coronation on Throne Day was a national holiday. It was the first national celebration following King Hussein's death. After their coronation, the king and queen prepared for their presentation to the people of Jordan. Queen Rania took her husband's hand and stepped into the back of a convertible limousine.

Jordan's Queen Rania Al Abdullah wore a traditional silk gown when she was crowned queen in 1999.

Rania — (RAH-nee-ah)
succeed — to take over for someone in a leadership position

THRONE DAY

The streets of Amman were filled with people waiting for the royal couple. Desert soldiers on camels, tribesmen on horses, and thousands of children packed the streets through Jordan's capital city. Red jeeps filled with security guards closely followed the royal couple's limousine.

King Abdullah and Queen Rania waved to the crowds from their limousine on Throne Day.

tribesman — a member of one of Jordan's many tribes that live in the desert

Queen Rania wore a shimmering gold gown. A diamond tiara sparkled in her dark hair. Beside her, Abdullah wore his formal white military uniform. As commander-in-chief of the Jordanian army, Abdullah's uniform now had a gold sash. The many medals he earned in the army shone in the sunlight. Jordanians tossed flowers and shouted "Long live Abdullah." They tried to touch the hands of the royal couple.

At the end of the parade, more than 800 guests waited to greet Rania and Abdullah at Raghdan Palace. The royal couple sat for portraits and greeted guests from all over the world. Despite her earlier worries, Rania was elegant, friendly, and calm. She was the very picture of royalty.

A BORROWED TIARA

Rania had to learn to be royal. When she needed a tiara for Throne Day, she borrowed one from her sister-in-law. The sparkling diamond tiara was worth about $2 million. Rania could not see spending so much money on something she would rarely wear.

GROWING UP IN
Kuwait

Rania Al-Yassin was born August 31, 1970, in Kuwait. Rania's father, Faisal, was a doctor who worked in Kuwait City. Her mother, Ilham, was a homemaker. Rania was the second of three children. Her sister, Dina, is three years older than Rania. One year after Rania was born, her brother, Majdi, joined the family.

Rania's parents wanted their children to receive a good education. They sent their children to the New English School, a private school in Kuwait City. Children of many nationalities attended this school. Faisal and Ilham wanted their children to learn about different cultures.

A SOLID EDUCATION

School meant changes for Rania and her siblings. The family spoke Arabic at home. At school, the courses were taught in English. Rania took a bus to school, and she wore a uniform. She earned good grades in science, math, and languages.

As a young girl, Rania (far left) attended New English School in Kuwait.

Lunchtime also meant changes. Most students ate hummus sandwiches. One day, a friend of Rania's brought a peanut butter and jelly sandwich. Rania thought this new sandwich was quite odd and rather disgusting. Until she tried it, that is. Her friend offered her a taste, and Rania took a small bite.

"Do you remember Scooby Doo, how Scooby would literally float off the ground at the thought of a Scooby snack? Well, that was my reaction to peanut butter and jelly. I thought it was heavenly," Rania remembered.

The school also had strict rules, which were sometimes hard for Rania to follow. Rania loved music and sometimes carried a small radio. She often listened to popular music on her breaks. But radios were against school rules. Rania hid the radio from her teachers, so she could still listen to her favorite songs.

hummus — a dip or sandwich spread made of chickpeas and sesame paste

WAR BRINGS CHANGE

Many summers, Rania and her siblings visited their relatives in the West Bank. This land sits west of Jordan near Israel. Rania's parents had left this troubled area when Jordan and Israel went to war in 1967. After six days of fighting, Israel took the West Bank from Jordan.

During these visits, Rania played chess and basketball with her cousins. But she also heard many stories from her relatives about people in Palestine who had lost their land and homes. The Israeli government gave the land to Israeli settlers. Her relatives had little say in their government under the Israelis.

OPERATION DESERT STORM (1991)

In August 1990, President Saddam Hussein of Iraq invaded Kuwait. He claimed that Kuwait's land belonged to Iraq. In January 1991, a group of 35 countries attacked Iraq's army and forced them to leave Kuwait. This conflict became known as Operation Desert Storm. The fighting in Kuwait forced Rania's family to leave their home in Kuwait City. The conflict, also known as the Gulf War, ended in February 1991.

Palestine — an ancient land west of Jordan

GOING AWAY TO UNIVERSITY

Rania took business administration classes at American University in Cairo, Egypt. She studied hard but also found time to go out with friends. In 1990, Rania and her friends watched on TV as a war broke out between Iraq and Kuwait. Rania worried that her parents would be hurt.

Rania's family escaped Kuwait City during the war, which became known as Operation Desert Storm. They moved to Amman, Jordan. When Rania graduated in 1991, she joined her family in Amman. She worked in banking and marketing.

Rania graduated with a degree in business administration from American University in Cairo, Egypt.

LOVE AT FIRST SIGHT

In January 1993, Rania was invited to a party given by Prince Abdullah's sister. Rania spent much of the evening talking to the prince. Later, Abdullah said he knew he wanted to marry Rania the first time he saw her. Yet, Rania wondered if a prince could fall in love with a commoner.

King Hussein hoped that his oldest son would find someone to marry. When he met Rania, the king knew she was the right woman for his son. In March 1993, King Hussein drove Abdullah to the Yassins' apartment. Abdullah asked Rania's father, Faisal, for her hand in marriage. Following tradition in Islam, King Hussein was present when Abdullah spoke with Rania's father. Faisal agreed, and Rania and Abdullah became engaged.

Rania and Abdullah dated for just six months before they were married in June 1993.

Islam — the religion of Muslims, based on the teachings of the prophet Muhammad

ROYAL WEDDING

On June 10, 1993, the young couple was married at Amman's royal palace. Rania beamed in her billowing white gown. Her long brown hair was swept up in a sparkling diamond tiara. Abdullah wore his blue military uniform covered with medals.

After the ceremony, hundreds of guests joined the couple at an elegant reception at the palace. A six-tiered wedding cake towered over the couple. An army friend of Abdullah's parachuted into the outdoor reception and cut the cake with a sword. Fireworks lit up the sky to celebrate the marriage. After the main party, Rania and Abdullah hosted a small party for their friends. The couple danced until dawn.

KING HUSSEIN (1935–1999)

King Hussein ruled Jordan for 47 years. Jordanians admired him for his efforts to bring peace to the Middle East. He was a popular king, both in Jordan and around the world.

3

FROM PRINCESS TO
Queen

After their marriage, Rania and Abdullah wanted a quieter home than the palace grounds. As a wedding gift, the king gave them a house on a hill overlooking Amman. The young couple settled into their new home and married life. Rania and Abdullah enjoyed relaxing by the pool or working in the gardens filled with flowering vines. At the end of the long driveway, guards protected the entrance to their home.

A year after they married, Rania and Abdullah had their first child. They named him Hussein after the king. Two years later, they had a baby girl named Iman. Toys soon filled the garden. Iman loved her swing set next to the pool.

Rania helps her daughters, Iman (back) and Salma (front), down a slide in the royal family's backyard.

A WORKING PRINCESS

The young couple devoted much of their time to work. They attended royal events with King Hussein and Queen Noor. Abdullah continued flying jets in the army. Rania began to work with charities and looked for ways to improve education in Jordan.

Weekends, however, were for family time. Abdullah and Rania made dinner together most evenings. Abdullah liked to barbecue. Rania enjoyed baking cakes and cooking. They both played with their children. The young couple relaxed in the evening and watched American TV shows.

Members of Jordan's royal family gathered at Raghdan Palace on Throne Day to honor King Abdullah (left) and Queen Rania.

Family is important to King Abdullah, Queen Rania, and their four children (from left) Princess Salma, Prince Hashem, Princess Iman, and Prince Hussein.

A NEW KING AND QUEEN

In 1998, King Hussein learned he had cancer. Though the king had the best care, he died in February 1999. Abdullah became king as soon as his father died. The nation held a three-month mourning period in honor of King Hussein. That June, Abdullah and Rania were officially crowned the new king and queen of Jordan.

After becoming queen, Rania still drove her children to school. The royal family continued to grow. In 2000, Princess Salma was born. In 2005, the royal couple welcomed a new son, Hashem. With four children, Rania worked hard to balance her family life and royal duties.

IMPROVING LIVES
IN Jordan

Queen Rania and King Abdullah have the same goals for Jordan. They want to add jobs and improve education. They publicly speak out in favor of peace in the Middle East. Rania focuses on improving the lives of women and children. The queen believes that educating women and girls is very important.

Jordan is a desert country. Only 10 percent of its land is good for farming. Most of Jordan's food is imported. With few natural resources, Jordan has high unemployment. Many of its people are poor.

WOMEN AND POVERTY

Rania founded the Jordan River Foundation (JRF) in 1995. The JRF helps rural women sell traditional handicrafts. The women weave textiles and make baskets. The project has created jobs for more than 500 women. The money they earn helps lift their families out of poverty.

Rania shows U.S. First Lady Laura Bush (center) work done through the Jordan River Foundation.

> "I am an Arab through and through, but I am also one who speaks the international language. I feel I do represent a large segment of women in the Arab world. I share with them their hopes and aspirations and the challenges they face."
>
> Interview with Queen Rania — May 2006

The JRF has new projects to help rural areas. Small villages have planted almond and fruit trees. Others raise camels and goats. The sale of milk and meat helps these villages make money.

Queen Rania also works to improve education for all people in Jordan. In 2007, Rania established Jordan's first children's museum to provide more educational opportunities for kids.

Rania helps children with artwork at the kingdom's Children's Museum in Amman.

Rania makes time in her busy schedule to meet with Jordanian citizens at hospitals.

HASHEMITE DYNASTY

King Abdullah II comes from a long line of royalty. The kings of Jordan are direct descendants of the Prophet Muhammad, who founded the religion of Islam. Hashemite kings ruled the holy city of Mecca from 1200 until 1925.

A COMPUTER IN EVERY CLASSROOM

In 2003, King Abdullah formed the Jordan Education Initiative to bring technology to Jordan's schools. With the help of international businesses, Jordan has 100 "Discovery Schools" that combine computer programs and teaching.

The program teaches science, math, Arabic, and English using computers. Rania hopes that someday, every classroom will have at least one computer. The Jordan Education Initiative has been a model for new projects in Palestine, Egypt, and India.

In 2006, Rania gave the first Queen Rania Award for Excellence in Education to the best teachers of Jordan. Teachers are important to the success of Jordanian students. Rania hopes that recognizing good teachers will encourage young people to pursue teaching as a career.

"As you educate a woman, you educate the family. If you educate the girls, you educate the future."

Interview with Queen Rania — May 2006

Rania often meets with students to talk about ways to improve technology in schools.

A VERY MODERN
Queen

King Abdullah and Queen Rania share a positive outlook about their country's future. Rania believes that most people in the world have the same hopes for their families. They want the best for their children.

Rania travels around the world to represent Jordan. Sometimes, she travels with her husband to meet presidents and prime ministers. Other times, she travels alone to represent her many charities. She even has her own jet to make her trips easier.

King Abdullah and Queen Rania often travel to different countries to meet with other world leaders.

THE PALESTINE PROBLEM

The fighting in Israel between the Palestinians and Israelis also affects Jordan. Many people from Palestine have come to Jordan as war refugees. Most have created a life for their families in Jordan. But many are still very poor.

Queen Rania is Palestinian by birth. She and the king have worked to promote a peaceful solution to the Palestinian need for a homeland. Rania and Abdullah hope that an independent Palestinian state might solve a major problem in the Middle East.

Rania (center) took part in an anti-terrorism march in Amman.

Rania is often invited to give speeches on world issues, such as peace, economics, and education.

Rania believes leaders must restore peace and a sense of security to young people. In 2006, Rania spoke of her hope for a peaceful solution. "For too long, people in our region have been weighed down with conflict and all its burdens," she said. "Their days are punctuated with images of despair and destruction, horror and heartbreak."

FASHIONABLE QUEEN

As queen, Rania is also known for her sense of style. She loves fashion and wears all types of clothes, from jeans and T-shirts to sequined gowns. Many have compared her fashion sense to the late Princess Diana.

But casual shopping trips to stores in Amman are not easy when you're the queen. Rania draws a large crowd wherever she goes, which creates problems for security guards and store owners. Instead, Rania shops at home. Designers send her "look books," so she can order what she wants. She also takes vacations to shop in London, New York, and Paris.

A NORMAL LIFE

At home, Queen Rania enjoys a relaxed family life. She jogs nearly every day, followed by a car full of bodyguards. The family loves to drive to the seaside palace at Aqaba. They water-ski, ride motorcycles in the desert, and swim.

She might be Queen Rania, but she prefers to be called by her name. "People call me queen but you know, that's not me. I'm Rania."

Despite her hectic schedule, Rania finds time to relax at Raghdan Palace in Amman.

Glossary

charity (CHAYR-uh-tee) — a group that raises money or collects goods to help people in need

commoner (KAH-muhn-ur) — someone who does not have royal ancestors

coronation (kor-uh-NAY-shun) — the ceremony in which a king or queen is crowned

hummus (HUHM-uhss) — a dip or sandwich spread made of chickpeas and sesame paste

Islam (ISS-luhm) — the religion of Muslims, based on the teachings of the prophet Muhammad

Palestine (PAH-luh-stine) — ancient land west of Jordan

poverty (PAW-vuhr-tee) — the state of being poor or without money

refugee (ref-yuh-JEE) — person forced to leave home because of war

succeed (suhk-SEED) — to take over for someone in a leadership position

textile (TEK-stile) — cloth that is created by weaving or knitting

tribesman (TRYBZ-man) — a member of one of Jordan's many tribes that live in the desert

Read More

Pundyk, Grace. *Welcome to Jordan.* Welcome to My Country. Milwaukee: Gareth Stevens, 2004.

Tait, Leia. *Queen Rania al-Abdullah.* Remarkable People. New York: Weigl, 2007.

Zuehlke, Jeffrey. *Jordan in Pictures.* Visual Geography. Minneapolis: Lerner, 2005.

Internet Sites

FactHound offers a safe, fun way to find Internet sites related to this book. All of the sites on FactHound have been researched by our staff.

Here's how:

1. Visit *www.facthound.com*
2. Choose your grade level.
3. Type in this book ID **1429619597** for age-appropriate sites. You may also browse subjects by clicking on letters, or by clicking on pictures and words.
4. Click on the **Fetch It** button.

FactHound will fetch the best sites for you!

Index